Five reasons why you'll love Mirabelle...

Mirabelle is magical and mischievous!

Mirabelle is half witch, half fairy, and totally naughty!

She loves making potions with her travelling potion kit!

Mirabelle loves sprinkling a sparkle of mischief wherever she goes!

She has a little baby dragon called Violet!

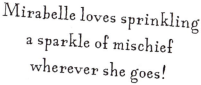

What would you like to find in a haunted house?

I want to go to a
ghost disco!
– Olivia

I'd find a haunted mirror that would
show me as a superhero with ice
cream shooting out of my hands!
– Amelia

I'd meet a skeleton and they'd
let me play the xylophone on
their rib bones.
– Avni

There would be a friendly
monster under the bed and
he'd tell me stories to help
me go to sleep.
– Georgie

I'd do some baking with a
witch and we'd cast a spell so
they never ran out!
– Isla

I'd play hide and seek
with a spooky cat.
– Valentina

Family Tree

My Mum
Seraphina Starspell

My brother
Wilbur Starspell

My Dad
Alvin Starspell

Me!
Mirabelle Starspell

Violet

Illustrated by Mike Love, based on
original artwork by Harriet Muncaster

OXFORD
UNIVERSITY PRESS

Great Clarendon Street, Oxford OX2 6DP
Oxford University Press is a department of the University of Oxford.
It furthers the University's objective of excellence in research, scholarship,
and education by publishing worldwide. Oxford is a registered trade mark
of Oxford University Press in the UK and in certain other countries

Database right Oxford University Press (maker)

First published in 2023

British Library Cataloguing in Publication Data

Data available

ISBN: 978-0-19-278872-6

1 3 5 7 9 10 8 6 4 2

Printed in China

Paper used in the production of this book is a natural,
recyclable product made from wood grown in sustainable forests.
The manufacturing process conforms to the environmental
regulations of the country of origin.

From the world of ISADORA MOON

MIRABELLE

and the Haunted House

Harriet Muncaster

OXFORD
UNIVERSITY PRESS

Chapter ONE

It was a *very* early Saturday morning in autumn. My brother Wilbur and I were having breakfast at the kitchen table when Mum ran into the room with her hair sticking up all over the place and soot smudges all over her face. Dad hurried in after her, his nose buried in a spellbook. My mum and dad own their own beauty business, concocting organic face creams, perfumes, and lipsticks. They spend a lot of time up in Mum's witch turret working on new lotions and potions.

'I'm sure I have some dried dragongrass flower petals *somewhere*!' said Mum, flinging open the cupboard under the sink and rummaging inside.

'It says you *can* substitute dragongrass flower petals for lizardgrass flower petals in potions,' said Dad. 'The end result just won't be as glittery.'

'Oh, but our new eyeshadow must be *glittery*!' said Mum. 'We absolutely need dragongrass flower petals!'

She began to throw things out of the cupboard until the whole kitchen floor was a mess of plastic bottles and cardboard cartons.

'There's none!' she cried, throwing her hands up in the air and looking defeated.

Then she noticed me and Wilbur sitting at the table watching her.

'Oh, good morning, my little witchlings!' she smiled. 'I didn't think you'd both be up so early!'

'The bangs woke me up,' said Wilbur.

'It sounded like fireworks!' I agreed.

Mum looked guilty.

'Oh dear,' she said. '*Sorry!*'

Dad came over and sat down at the table.

He looked exhausted.

'Mum and I got a bit carried away experimenting with new potions early this morning,' he said. 'There might have been a few little *explosions*.'

'We're trying to make the perfect berry-purple eyeshadow,' explained Mum.

'And we wanted to get our work done as early as possible this morning so that we could all spend time together as a family today!'

'It *is* a lovely crisp and sunny day!' said Dad, glancing out of the window wistfully. My dad is a fairy, and he loves sunshine and nature. 'Perfect picnic weather! It might be our last chance to have one before the weather gets colder.'

'Well, it's *quite* a nice day,' said Mum pickily. My mum is a witch, and she prefers things a little more gloomy and atmospheric.

'Ooh! *Can* we go on a picnic?' I asked hopefully.

Mum and Dad looked at each other worriedly.

'I'm not sure . . .' said Mum.

'Our deadline for the eyeshadow is tomorrow,' said Dad. 'Unfortunately, I think Mum and I need to fly all the way to the witch market to buy a dragongrass flower today. We need it urgently.'

'I'm so sorry, my witchlings,' said Mum. 'Maybe we can have a picnic tomorrow instead? It looks like it's going to be *lovely* weather tomorrow! Stormy!'

Dad gazed out of the window. He looked very disappointed.

I felt disappointed too. A picnic would have been fun!

'Hmm,' said Wilbur. He twirled his spoon around in his bowl of fairy flakes for a moment and then he said, '*I* thought dragongrass flowers grew in the wild! Why do you need to go all the way to the witch market to get some?'

'Dragongrass flowers are hard to find in the wild,' said Mum. 'It will be much more reliable to just go and buy one.'

I felt myself perk up.

'But we have Violet!' I said, reaching down to pet my little purple dragon. 'Dragons are known to be very good at sniffing out dragongrass flowers. She could help! I think we could easily find a wild dragongrass flower with Violet's help!'

'Or even *without* her help,' said Wilbur, puffing out his chest. '*I'm* very good at finding things. I'm sure I could find one even without Violet!'

I gave Wilbur a cross nudge under the table.

'Oww!' wailed Wilbur. 'Mum, Dad, Mirabelle's *attacking* me!'

'Don't attack your brother, Mirabelle,' said Mum, wearily.

'Oh, pleeeease can we go on a dragongrass flower hunt today?' I begged.

'We could all go together *and* have a picnic at the same time!'

'That does sound like a rather nice idea,' said Dad, his fairy wings perking up happily.

Mum sighed.

'Well, all right then,' she relented. 'Let's go on a dragongrass flower hunt. I suppose I could rush to the night market

tonight if we don't find any. I'll quickly make us a picnic, shall I?'

Wilbur, Dad, and I looked at each other in horror. We all know what Mum's idea of a picnic would be! Spider sandwiches and jellied insects on sticks. *No thanks!* Neither Wilbur nor I had inherited Mum's love of witch food. We prefer fairy food.

'*I'll* make the picnic,' said Dad quickly.
We all breathed a sigh of relief.

An hour or so later we were all standing by
the door and ready to go. I had found my
backpack and filled it with all the things I
might need for a dragongrass flower hunt:
a magnifying glass, some binoculars, and, of
course, my travelling potion kit.

We left the house and all rose up into
the air—Mum, Wilbur, and me on our
broomsticks, and Dad fluttering along
beside us on his fairy wings. (Wilbur and
I didn't inherit Dad's fairy wings, which is
something I always feel a bit disappointed
about.)

It was a beautiful day, and down below us the trees were all starting to turn red and gold. I felt all light and sparkly as we soared over the town and then the forest and the fields beyond. Soon we came to a place where there were some big hills covered in trees. There was a stream running through the valley between the hills. It looked like a golden ribbon glinting in the light of the low autumn sun.

'This looks like a perfect place for picnicking!' said Dad. 'Very wild! Hopefully we will find a dragongrass flower here!'

'Yes,' agreed Mum and she began to point her broomstick downwards, heading for a shady patch underneath some trees, right next to the stream.

I landed on the ground next to Wilbur, and Mum laid out the rug.

'Let's start the picnic!' I said, pulling the hamper towards me and opening it up. Inside were lots of sandwiches with different fillings, cut into star and moon shapes, a box of carrot and cucumber sticks, and a big cherry and chocolate cake

covered in swirls of glittery fairy icing.
Mum wrinkled her nose.

'*Where* are the jellied bugs?' she
asked.

'I put them in a separate container,'
said Dad. 'I didn't want them er . . .
contaminating our food. It's not lunchtime
yet anyway. Close the lid of the picnic
basket, Mirabelle!'

'*What!?*' I stared at Dad in dismay.

'It's only ten o'clock.' said Dad. 'Still
two hours until lunchtime at least!'

'But Dad!' I said, feeling my tummy
rumbling. 'We've all been up for *hours*
remember! It *feels* like lunchtime!'

'We'll have more energy for finding

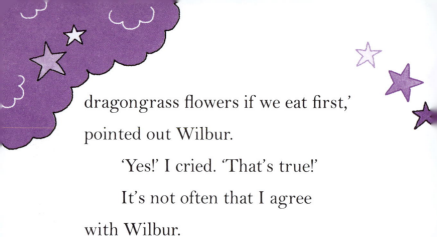

dragongrass flowers if we eat first,'
pointed out Wilbur.

'Yes!' I cried. 'That's true!'

It's not often that I agree
with Wilbur.

Dad sighed.

'Well, I suppose we *could* start the picnic,' he said.

Wilbur and I fell onto the picnic basket, taking everything out as fast as we could and piling it onto plates. Mum found her box of witch food and bit into a spider roll.

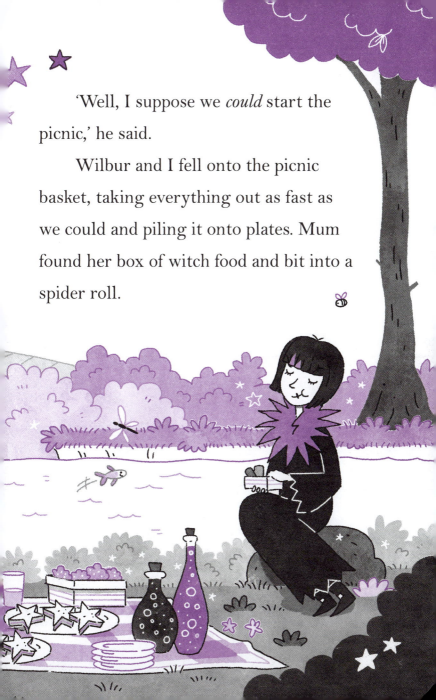

'Yum!' I said, lying down on the rug once I had finished.

'Yum,' agreed Mum, lying down next to me and pulling Dad down with her.

The three of us stared up at the sky. Dad yawned.

'I suppose we'd better get on with finding this dragongrass flower,' he said.

'I suppose so,' yawned Mum, closing her eyes.

'Maybe in a minute,' said Dad.

'Mmm,' said Mum.

Then . . . silence.

All I could hear was the trickling
of the stream nearby and rustling of the
crispy orange leaves in the trees.

I sat up on the rug and stared at
my parents.

They were both asleep!

I looked around for Wilbur.

Where was he?

I hadn't even noticed him wander off.

Suddenly, I spotted Wilbur in the distance. He was with *my* dragon, Violet, and they were both bent over, peering closely at the flowers.

Chapter TWO

Annoyance zinged through me, and I stood up and brushed the crumbs from my skirt.

I knew what Wilbur was up to! He wanted to be the first to find a dragongrass flower!

Leaving Mum and Dad snoozing, I ran away from the rug and over to my brother.

'Wilbur!!' I exclaimed.

'Oh hi, Mirabelle,' said Wilbur, a little sheepishly. 'I just thought I'd get started on the dragongrass hunt.'

'You should have waited for me!' I said.

'Sorry,' shrugged Wilbur.

But he didn't look sorry at all.

He looked *sneaky*!

It made me feel cross.

'Come here, Violet!' I said, beckoning to her. 'Come with *me*! Let's go and hunt for dragongrass on our own! We'll find some before Wilbur!'

'Stay with *me*, Violet!' said Wilbur. 'I've got a biscuit for you!'

He reached into his pocket and
brought out a foil-wrapped chocolate
biscuit.

I gasped.

Violet *loves* chocolate biscuits! She
looked at me and then she looked at
Wilbur. And then she flapped her little
purple leathery wings and flew up to
land on Wilbur's shoulder.

'WILBUR!' I shouted,
stamping my foot. 'You
planned this all along!'

'I can't help where Violet
wants to go,' said Wilbur smugly.

I stomped away from them both,
towards a cluster of trees nearby. Angry

fireworks exploded within me.

Fine! Let Wilbur and Violet look
for a dragongrass flower on their own,
I thought. I didn't need them! I would
find one *myself*! Feeling a fresh burst of
energy, I moved into the trees and began
to look along the mossy ground for some
dragongrass flowers. I saw lots of colourful
toadstools and lots of crunchy leaves on the
ground. But no dragongrass flower.

I moved further into the cluster of
trees. Everything seemed a lot darker now
than it had a few minutes ago. I looked
up at the sky through the leaves and was
surprised to see that it had suddenly turned
quite grey and cloudy. Little spots of rain

began to fall and the wind picked up, whistling through the trees.

I shivered. Maybe the stormy weather that Mum had mentioned that morning was arriving earlier than expected! Still, I was determined not to let it stop me from finding a dragongrass flower. I really, *really* wanted to find one before Wilbur! Especially now that he had been so mean!

I walked even further into the trees. Then I stopped and stared.

My heart soared.

There was something bright
and purple peeping out from behind a
tree trunk.

Something with bright pink
lightning-bolt shapes on its violet petals.

Could it be . . . ?

Could it?!

I ran forwards and then punched the air with my fist.

'Yesssss!'

A single dragongrass flower, looking bright and cheerful against the gloomy backdrop of the trees! It was covered all over with raindrops that looked like tiny diamonds in the light. It looked so pretty that I felt bad taking it from its wild home. But Dad *had* said it would be OK to pick just one for the potion. And I knew he would save some of its seeds and come back here to replant them.

I kneeled down and reached out to pick the dragongrass flower. Everything else around me seemed to disappear as I

stared at it in wonder. My hand was just
about to close around its stalk when—

BOOOMPH!

A foot came stamping down on it from above, spattering tiny droplets everywhere.

I *recognized* that shoe!

That horrid *horrid* shoe!

I looked up.

'WILBUR!!!' I screamed.

Wilbur jumped backwards in shock and Violet flapped her wings worriedly in the air.

'YOU DID THAT ON PURPOSE!' I shouted, leaping to my feet and feeling tears begin to prick at my eyes. I stared down at the poor dragongrass flower which was now stamped down into the sludgy mud.

Crushed!

Ruined!

Mum and Dad would never be able to use it for their potion now!

'Uh, sorry!' said Wilbur, turning bright red. 'I didn't see it there!'

'You *did* see it!' I shouted at him. 'I know you did! You must have been following me!'

'I didn't see it!' stuttered Wilbur. But I could tell he was lying. His face always goes bright red when he lies.

I wiped the tears from my eyes and sniffed.

'I really am sorry, Mirabelle,' said Wilbur, looking very guilty now and shuffling his feet about on the ground. 'I—uh . . .'

I glared at him furiously.

It felt like the weather was furious too. The rain started to fall down harder and harder, and the wind whipped my hair into a frenzy. Suddenly, there was a huge crack of thunder overhead and the whole sky lit up with a flash of lightning. Violet

squealed in fright and zipped off into
the trees. She hates thunderstorms.

'That's the wrong way, Violet!'
I called. But Violet just kept flying,
her little purple tail disappearing into
the leaves.

I began to run after her, keeping my eyes trained on her tail. I pushed through the wet leaves and branches, following Violet deeper into the copse until suddenly the trees opened out into a clearing. Violet stopped in mid-air, flapping her wings in surprise.

I stopped too.

And then I heard Wilbur stop just behind me.

Because, in the middle of the clearing, there was a little house! It didn't seem like anyone lived inside it because the door was wide open and hanging off its hinges. The whole thing looked very old and run down.

'Ooh!' I said, forgetting about the dragongrass flower for a moment. 'A secret house! Let's explore quickly before we go back to Mum and Dad!'

Wilbur shivered.

'*I'm* not going in!' he said. 'And you shouldn't either, Mirabelle. It looks exactly like the sort of spooky house you'd read about in a fairy tale! There's probably an evil witch inside who wants to put us in the oven and bake us into gingerbread people.'

I laughed.

'Oh don't be silly, Wilbur!' I said. 'And anyway, *I'm* a witch! I've got my travelling potion kit with me in my backpack. I'll just turn *her* into a gingerbread person!'

'I still don't think we should,' said Wilbur. 'It might be haunted!'

I shrugged, although Wilbur *was* starting to make me feel a bit nervous.

'So what?' I said. 'I'm not scared of ghosts! Cousin Isadora has a very friendly ghost called Oscar who lives in her attic, remember? He's not scary at all!'

Even so, I started to feel prickles run all the way up and down my arms. Now that I looked at it more, the house *did* seem to be very dark and empty and abandoned. I was starting to feel like maybe I didn't want to go and explore inside it after all.

Suddenly, there was another crack of thunder and a flash of bright silver lightning, and Violet zoomed forwards towards the house, disappearing through the front door.

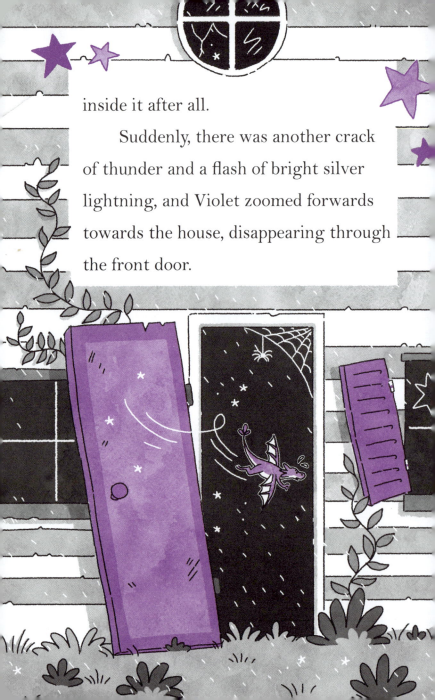

'Mirabelle!' cried Wilbur. 'You should have grabbed her while she was next to us!'

'*You* should have grabbed her!' I argued.

'She's *your* dragon!' said Wilbur.

'Well, *you* lured her away from me today with chocolate biscuits!' I replied. 'So she's your responsibility too!'

We both stared at the house.

'Let's just run in quickly,' suggested Wilbur. 'And fetch her out together. It won't take long.'

I took a deep breath. There didn't seem to be another option, unless I wanted to leave Violet here in the middle of the wood. Alone.

I could never do that to her!

Poor Violet!

'OK,' I said reluctantly.

'OK,' said Wilbur.

Together we walked towards the house.

Chapter
THREE

Wilbur and I stopped in front of the
gaping open front door and peered inside.
It looked shadowy and smelled musty.
Small shivers ran up and down my spine.

'You go in first, Mirabelle,' said
Wilbur.

'*You* go in first!' I said. 'You're older!'

'You're younger,' said Wilbur.

'That doesn't even make sense!'
I cried.

Big brothers can be *infuriating*
sometimes.

I stepped over the threshold. I was
so annoyed at Wilbur that I had forgotten
to be frightened for a moment.

'*I'm* not a scaredy cat!' I said,
sticking my tongue out at him.

'Well nor am I then!' retorted
Wilbur, following me into the house.

It was very dark in the hallway so
I got out my little potion kit and poured
a bit of amethyst crystal powder into my
hands. Blowing onto it, I whispered a
magic spell.

Crickle crackle, flicker fright.
Light this place up, nice and bright!

Immediately a little purple flame
burst into life, hovering just above my
hands. It wasn't hot, just very bright,
and it sent dark shadows dancing all over
the walls of the house, making it look as
though things were moving.

'Hello!' I called in a slightly wobbly
voice, just in case someone was there.

Nothing.

But outside the storm continued
to rage.

'Let's find Violet quickly!' whispered Wilbur. 'It's creepy here! And it smells funny!'

He pushed a window open with a loud long *creeeeak*. A gust of cold wet air blew in, extinguishing the flame in my hands.

'*Wilbur!*' I hissed, feeling annoyed

once more. '*Look* what you've done! It's all dark again now!'

'I didn't do it on purpose!' said Wilbur defensively. 'I was trying to get rid of the musty old smell!'

'You *did* do that on purpose!' I huffed.

'I *didn't*!' replied Wilbur.

'Did!' I replied.

SLAM!

Wilbur and I both jumped in fright.

What was that?

A sound from upstairs!

'Let's leave,' whispered Wilbur. 'There's someone here!'

'But what about Violet?' I said. 'We can't abandon her! Maybe that was *Violet* making a noise!'

Wilbur's eyes were big and round in the dim darkness.

'I don't like it here, Mirabelle,' he said. 'I think we should go and find Mum and Dad!'

'Well, *I* think we should be brave

and find Violet first.' I said, not feeling very brave at all, but determined not to let Wilbur win. 'Come on, let's go upstairs.'

'Upstairs?' Wilbur stared at me in horror.

'I'm going to look,' I said.

'Well, I'm not staying down here alone!' replied Wilbur, and he reluctantly followed me up the creaky, dark staircase. With every step, I felt more and more afraid, but I kept forcing myself to go further. I had to find Violet. I hated the idea of her being frightened.

I reached the top of the stairs and crept down a hallway, peering into one of the bedrooms. Inside there was an old wardrobe standing against the wall and a bed with no mattress on it. The window was wide open and swinging to and fro on its hinges.

I breathed a sigh of relief.

'It was just the window slamming, Wilbur!' I said, running over to it and pulling it shut.

'I *knew* it would just be something like that!' said Wilbur.

'No you didn't!' I said, as I made sure the window was latched properly.

'Yes I did!' he replied.

I turned back round.

And screamed.

'ARGH!'

'Whaaa?' shouted Wilbur, leaping backwards.

'YOU!' I yelled. 'You're right in my face, Wilbur! Don't creep up behind me like that! You scared me.'

'Oh,' said Wilbur.

And then he *laughed*.

I felt crosser with him than ever.

Why oh why was he being SO horrible today? First he stole Violet from me, then he stomped on my flower! *Then*, he blew out my purple flame, and now he was trying to make me jump! I needed to get away from Wilbur and out of this house as soon as possible!

'Let's just find Violet,' I said huffily. 'And leave!'

I sprinkled some more amethyst powder onto my hands and created another purple flame.

'OK, Wilbur,' I said, our faces flickering in the purple glow. 'Let's both be really quiet and listen out for Violet.'

We both stood in the bedroom with our ears pricked. Sometimes, Violet makes noises on the floorboards with her claws. But I couldn't hear anything like that. Just the wailing of the wind outside.

'Sounds ghostly!' whispered Wilbur. 'If only there *was* a ghost around to help us! That would be good, wouldn't it, Mirabelle?'

'Shh, Wilbur!' I said.

But Wilbur ignored me.

'OooooOOOOoooo,' he moaned.

I stared at him angrily.

'OOooo!' he said again.

'*What* are you doing?' I asked.

But Wilbur didn't reply. He just kept

making little ghost-like noises.

Suddenly, something inside me just broke. I couldn't *bear* even one more minute with my annoying brother.

'ARGHHH!!!!' I screeched at him, throwing my hands up in the air in frustration so that the purple flame fell onto the floor. 'I wish you'd just DISAPPEAR!'

There was a huge bang as the purple flame hit the floor. Lots of sparkly smoke and then . . .

Nothing.

I stared ahead of me as the smoke cleared.

Wilbur was gone!

Chapter FOUR

I felt my heart start to race.

'Wilbur?' I called. 'Wilbur! Where are you?'

There was no reply.

I looked down at my hands which still had traces of amethyst dust all over them and started to shake. Could my flame spell have *somehow* made my brother disappear?

I hadn't meant to throw it on the floor!
I hadn't even really meant what I'd said
about him disappearing.

Well, I had sort of meant it in that
one tiny moment.

But not *really*.

I had just been so angry!

'WILBUR!' I called out one last time.
'This is not the time to be playing silly
tricks on me!'

Nothing. Just silence and the wailing
of the wind.

The house felt so much spookier
without Wilbur there.

'Oh no!' I whispered into the gloom.
My heart was beating so hard that it felt

like it might burst out of my chest.

What had I done?!

I had made my brother vanish into thin air!

Was there a way to bring him back? I had no idea! I didn't even know how I had managed to cast the spell in the first place, so how was I supposed to know which spell to use to make it right again?!

This was a disaster!

What would Mum and Dad say?

Maybe Wilbur was gone forever! And it was all my fault!

I sat down on the floor in despair, hugging my knees tightly to my chest, rocking backwards and forwards with panic.

'Oh help!' I squeaked. 'Oh help!
Oh help!'

'Hello?' came a voice.

I looked up, feeling hopeful for just a
split-second.

'Wilbur?' I said.

But it didn't sound like Wilbur's voice.

There must be someone else in the house!

I stood up, my knees quivering, reaching out for my potion kit in case I should need it.

'Hello?' said the voice again, and

suddenly a little white shape came puffing out of the wardrobe.

I breathed a sigh of relief.

It was just a ghost!

A small sweet one with a big flouncy bow tied in her silvery hair.

'Oh, thank goodness!' I said out loud. 'Hello! Who are you?'

'I'm Luna,' said the little ghost. 'I've been watching you since you came into the house. I didn't want to show myself as you both seemed a bit . . . angry. But now you look sad, I thought I'd better try and help! I'm sorry I didn't reply when your brother was trying to talk to me.'

'What?!' I said. 'My brother was trying to talk to you?'

'I thought so!' shrugged Luna. 'You know, when he was doing all that "OooOOOoo," stuff. Most people think that's how ghosts talk. It's not by the way. Well, mostly not.'

'Oh,' I said, starting to feel bad.
'I just thought Wilbur was being *really*
annoying.'

'I think he was just trying to help,'
said Luna.

'Oh dear!' I said. 'Now I feel even
worse about making him disappear!
Oh, what am I going to do?!
My brother is *gone*! Maybe
forever!'

'Hmm!' said Luna,
'I'm sure he can't really
have disappeared! He
could just be hiding or
something! That's the kind
of thing *my* brother would do.'

'You have a brother?' I asked her. 'Is he a ghost too?'

'Oh yes,' said Luna. 'We both live here together. Just us! So we used to argue a lot. Just like you and Wilbur! But being stuck here together for so many years, we learned to see things from each other's point of view a bit more. It helps a lot. You should try it!'

I felt defensive.

'Wilbur and I don't argue!' I said. 'We just—'

But then I stopped.

That was a lie.

Wilbur and I did argue.

We argued a *lot*.

'I also need to find my dragon Violet,' I said, changing the subject. 'Did you see a little purple dragon fly into the house?'

'No,' replied Luna, 'but I'll help you find both of them if you like?'

'I'd love that!' I said. 'Thank you!'

Everything felt a bit lighter and brighter now that I had Luna by my side. As we both searched the house, even the storm outside seemed to die down a little. Luna and I went from room to room, looking in cobwebby cupboards and creaky drawers, under the bed-frame, and even inside the rusty old bath! We were able to go quite

fast because Luna was able to poke her
head into cabinets without even opening
them, which was very useful!

'Not in here,' she kept saying. 'Not
in here!'

'Oh dear,' I said, starting to lose hope. 'He doesn't seem to be anywhere! Maybe I *really did* make him disappear!'

Luna didn't reply. She bit her lip and looked a bit worried, which just made me feel more worried!

'It *is* strange,' she said. 'I think we've looked in every hiding place now. I guess it's *possible* that you did somehow make him disappear. Witch magic can be tricksy!'

My heart began to race with panic once again. For a little while I had started to believe that Luna was right. That Wilbur was just hiding somewhere in the house. But we hadn't found him *anywhere*!

He must have really and properly vanished!

'And we still haven't found Violet either!' I wailed, putting my head in my hands.

Neither of us said anything for a moment.

'I know!' exclaimed Luna suddenly. 'Let's try outside!' She led me towards the back door of the house and opened it. Golden sunshine flooded into the old tumbledown kitchen. It was clear that the storm had passed.

I stared out into the back garden.

My heart leaped into my throat.

'Look!' I cried.

Kneeling down in the middle of the grass, surrounded by autumn leaves and pumpkins, and with Violet in his arms, was Wilbur!

Chapter FIVE

'Oh, *Wilby!*' I shouted, running over to him and giving him and Violet a huge, relieved hug.

'Uh, hi Mirabelle,' said Wilbur, sounding surprised.

'I thought you were lost forever!' I said. 'I thought I had made you disappear when I threw the firelight down on the floor!'

Then I started to feel cross.

'Why did you leave me alone inside the creepy house?' I asked.

'I didn't mean to,' said Wilbur.

'Yes you di—' I began and then stopped myself. Maybe I should listen to Wilbur's point of view before starting an argument.

'When the firelight exploded,' Wilbur said, 'I ran out of the room. I was going to come back in once the smoke had cleared but then I bumped into a ghost in the hallway! Would you believe it, Mirabelle? A ghost!'

'Well—' I began.

'He's called Jupiter,' said Wilbur, 'and he's really friendly! We just got chatting and then he helped me find Violet! She was out here all along, hiding among the pumpkins!'

Now I looked around I started to

notice the garden properly. There were vegetables, toadstools, and clumps of herbs everywhere! The pumpkins must have made a perfect hiding place for little Violet.

Wilbur looked a bit sheepish now.

'I'm sorry for stamping on your dragongrass flower, Mirabelle,' he said. 'I *did* mean to do it and I felt terrible afterwards. I just wanted to be the first to find one! But I shouldn't ever have stomped on the one you found.'

I felt my heart start to glow. It's not often that Wilbur apologizes to me and I could tell he truly felt really bad for upsetting me. Suddenly, I didn't even care that much about the dragongrass flower.

'I didn't mean to do any of the other things though, by the way,' continued Wilbur. 'Like making your firelight go out or scaring you by the window. I was

trying to help by making ghost noises!'

'That's OK, Wilbur,' I replied graciously. 'I'm sorry too, for saying that I wished you would disappear. I don't really . . . well, *most* of the time.' I added under my breath.

'Hey!' cried Wilbur, nudging me with his elbow.

We both laughed.

It felt good to laugh with my brother. Especially now that we had found Violet and the sun was shining again!

'Oh look!' said Wilbur suddenly. 'There's Jupiter!'

He pointed across the garden to a silvery shape hovering above one of the flower beds, watching us. He had a pair of pruning shears in his silvery hands. I waved at him and he waved back. Then he put the pruning shears down and floated towards us. As he did so I noticed another silvery shape peep her head out of the back door. It was Luna! She glided out of the house and across the flowers to join us.

'Oh! That must be Jupiter's sister.' said Wilbur. 'He said he had a sister.'

'It is,' I said. 'She's my new friend.'

'*You* met a ghost too?' asked Wilbur, sounding disappointed.

'I did,' I said, trying not to sound smug. There was no point starting another argument with my brother.

The four of us gathered together in the middle of the garden.

'It's very beautiful here,' I said.

'It is,' agreed Wilbur.

'We both just really love gardening!' said Jupiter, shrugging.

'There's not much else to do,' added Luna. 'We have a lot of time on our hands.

And we don't have many visitors.'

I felt a bit sorry for Luna and Jupiter then.

'*We'll* make sure we come back and visit you!' I said. 'I'll introduce you to my parents! Dad will love your garden. He's a fairy and loves anything to do with nature!'

'Mum will love it too,' added Wilbur. 'It looks like it's bursting with magical witchy plants!'

'Oh, it is!' cried Luna.

'Do you have any dragongrass flowers by any chance?' I asked, hopefully. 'We actually came here specially to look for one.'

'Oh yes!' replied Luna. 'We've grown a whole patch of them at the bottom of the garden! Do you want to see?'

Wilbur and I looked at each other excitedly.

'Yes please!' we both said.

Luna and Jupiter led us down a little grassy path between the wildflowers. We went through a leafy arch and right down to the end of the garden where there was a ramshackle wooden fence.

'Here!' said Luna, pointing.

Growing up in front of the fence was a whole patch of beautiful, purple dragongrass flowers with bright pink lightning-bolt patterns on their petals.

Violet immediately zoomed towards them and stuck her snout into the flowers.

'Oh *wow*!' I exclaimed.

'*Amazing*,' said Wilbur.

We both looked at Luna and Jupiter.

'Is there *any* chance we could have just one to take home?' I asked. 'For a potion.'

'Of course!' beamed Jupiter. 'We'd love to help!'

He floated away to find the pruning shears.

'Just make sure you save some of the seeds,' said Luna. 'And replant them somewhere else. To make up for the one you took from nature.'

'The two we took,' I thought inside my head, thinking about the poor dragongrass flower that Wilbur had squashed earlier. But I forced myself not to say anything.

It would only start an argument. And Wilbur *had* apologized.

Jupiter returned with the pruning shears and snipped one of the flowers out from the patch, handing it to me and Wilbur.

'Thank you!' I said. 'Thank you so much!'

Luna and Jupiter looked pleased.

'I wish we could stay longer,' I said. 'But I think we'd better start getting back to Mum and Dad now. They'll be wondering where we are. We'll come and visit again soon though!'

'That would be wonderful!' beamed Luna.

Without thinking, I tried to give her a hug but my arms just went straight through her! She felt like a chilly mist, and prickles ran all the way up and down my spine.

'Oops!' I said.

'It's OK!' laughed Luna.

Chapter SIX

Wilbur and I waved goodbye to our new friends and walked away from the house, away from the clearing and back through the forest with Violet fluttering along beside us. Now that the sun was out again, everything seemed so much less ominous, and the grass glittered all over with raindrops, like little jewels.

'There you are!' said Mum, running towards us when we emerged out of the wood. 'We were starting to get worried!'

'We assumed you were sheltering somewhere nearby from the storm,' said

Dad. 'Mum and I were happily snoozing on the picnic blanket when we suddenly woke up completely soaked!'

'Drenched!' agreed Mum, squeezing out her dress.

'We were just in the forest,' I said.

'There's a house in there!' said Wilbur.

'With two little ghosts in it,' I said. 'We made friends with them. They'd love to meet you!'

'Oh?' said Mum. 'Well, I'd love to meet them too. But not before I've found a dragongrass flower. Time is running out. Dad and I didn't mean to fall asleep! We must start our search!'

She wrung her hands, looking worried.

Wilbur and I smiled at each other.

'You don't need to worry, Mum,' I said, bringing my hand out from behind my back. 'We found one for you!'

104

'You did?!'

Mum and Dad both

stared at the dragongrass flower in

amazement as I held it up for them to

see, the luminous purple petals reflecting

brightly in their eyes.

'Oh, but this is wonderful!' said

Mum.

'Fantastic!' agreed Dad, looking

relieved. 'We'll be able to finish our

potion tonight!' He took the flower

from me and cradled it gently in his

hands.

'This means,' said Mum 'that

we can stay here and *relax* for the

rest of the day! I'll do a spell to dry the picnic rug.'

'Whoopee!' yelled Wilbur. 'I want to eat more picnic!'

'And I'd like to go swimming in the stream,' said Dad.

Mum smiled.

'We can do all those things,' she said, happily. 'And maybe later we can go into the little wood and meet your new friends?'

'Yes!' I said. 'I'm sure they would love that!'

'They would,' agreed Wilbur. '*I* was the one who discovered them you know!'

I frowned at him.

'No you weren't,' I said. '*I* found Luna!'

'But I found Jupiter first,' said Wilbur.

'Only by a few minutes!' I said, starting to feel cross. 'And—'

But then I stopped and closed my eyes, taking a deep breath like Mum does sometimes when Wilbur and I are arguing. I remembered what Luna had said about taking time to see the other person's point of view. I supposed that *technically* Wilbur had met a ghost first, and if he was determined to be annoying about it then . . .

I opened my eyes, and with a great amount of effort, I smiled sweetly at my brother.

'OK, Wilbur,' I said. 'You did find a ghost before me today.'

Wilbur looked shocked. His mouth fell open.

Mum put her hand on my shoulder.

'Well done, Mirabelle,' she said in surprise. 'That was very mature of you!'

I had to stop my mouth from twitching into a smug smile.

'Well, I'm just trying to be a bit kinder to my brother,' I said.

Wilbur frowned, looking a bit annoyed.

'*Well*,' he said after a moment. '*I'm* trying to be kinder to my sister.'

Violet looked at us both and gave a disbelieving snort.

'That's wonderful!' said Dad, beaming.

'*Yes*,' said Mum, raising an arched black eyebrow.

Wilbur and I followed our parents back towards the picnic rug. As we walked Wilbur nudged me with his elbow.

'*I'm* going to be the kindest,' he muttered.

'*I'm* going to be the kindest,' I whispered back.

'No, *I* am,' said Wilbur.

'*I* am,' I replied.

'*I* am.'

'*I* am.'

'*I* am.'

Turn the page
for some
mischievous
things to make
and do!

How to make your own haunted house

Ghosts Luna and Jupiter live in a spooky haunted house—here's how to make your own!

What you will need:

- ★ Cardboard boxes (e.g. cereal boxes, shoe boxes)
- ★ Cardboard
- ★ Toilet roll tubes/other cardboard tubes
- ★ Paint
- ★ Felt-tip pens
- ★ Craft glue/PVA glue
- ★ Glue stick
- ★ Sellotape/packing tape
- ★ Scissors
- ★ A grown-up assistant to help

Method

1. Make a plan. What kind of haunted house do you want to build? Draw a sketch or make a list of the rooms you want to include.

2. Gather materials. Collect cereal boxes, shoe boxes, toilet roll tubes, and other craft materials you may need.

3. Build the structure. Use cardboard boxes to create the walls of the haunted house, and fix them together using glue or sticky tape. You could make turrets out of cardboard tubes.

4. Cut out windows and doors as needed. Make sure a grown-up helps you with this. Alternatively, you could draw them on.

5. Paint or decorate the outside of your house.

6. When the outside is dry, move on to the inside! Using felt-tip pens, paint, or other materials, colour in your walls and add spooky decorations.

7. If you have doll's house furniture you could put this inside, or make/draw your own!

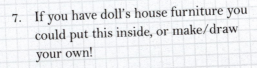

How to make your own ghost

This friendly little ghost blows in the wind—if you make lots they will make great Halloween decorations!

What you will need:

* White paper
* Empty toilet roll tubes
* Glue
* Hole punch
* Scissors
* Ribbon
* Strips of crepe paper
* String
* Black pen or paint
* Googly eyes
* A grown-up assistant to help

Method

1. Roll the white paper around the toilet roll tube and stick it down with glue. (White paper cups also work really well for this.)

2. Draw a ghost face using black pen or paint. You could use googly eyes to give your ghost even more character! Will you make them scary or friendly?

3. Use the hole punch to punch holes around the bottom of your tube.

4. Thread a length of ribbon through a hole and tie a knot in the end to secure.

5. Repeat until you have gone all around the tube.

6. Alternatively, cut lengths of crepe paper and glue these to the bottom of your tube.

7. Use the hole punch to put a hole on either side at the top of the tube.

8. Thread the string through, then tie the ends together to form a loop.

9. Make as many as you like—you could give them different faces.

10. Hang your little ghosts in a tree or over a doorway and watch them bob in the wind!

Ghost biscuits

Here's how to make delicious ghost biscuits!

Ingredients

For biscuits:

- ★ 100g unsalted butter, softened at room temperature
- ★ 100g caster sugar
- ★ 1 free-range egg, lightly beaten
- ★ 1 tsp vanilla extract
- ★ 275g plain flour

For decoration:

- ★ 400g icing sugar
- ★ 3–4 tbsp water
- ★ 2–3 drops food colouring
- ★ Edible glitter

Equipment:

- Baking tray
- Greaseproof paper
- Mixing bowl
- Wooden spoon
- Fork
- Sieve
- Rolling pin
- Ghost-shaped cookie cutters
- Wire rack
- Knife
- A grown-up assistant to help

Method

1. Preheat the oven to 190°C/Gas 5.

2. Line a baking tray with greaseproof paper.

3. Cream the butter and sugar together in a bowl until pale, light and fluffy.

4. Beat the egg.

5. Add the beaten egg and vanilla extract, a little at a time, until well combined.

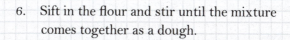

6. Sift in the flour and stir until the mixture comes together as a dough.

7. Lightly flour your clean working surface.

8. Roll the dough out to a thickness of around 1cm.

9. Use the cookie cutters to cut out ghost shapes, and carefully place onto the baking tray. Alternatively, ask a grown-up to help you cut out the shapes by hand.

10. Gather the trimmings and repeat steps 8 and 9 until there is no dough left.

11. Bake the biscuits for 8–10 minutes, or until pale golden-brown.

12. Set aside to harden for 5 minutes, then cool on a wire rack.

For the icing:

1. Sift the icing sugar into a large mixing bowl and stir in enough water to create a smooth mixture.

2. Stir in the food colouring (add a tiny amount at a time—a little goes a long way!)

3. Carefully spread the icing onto the biscuits using a knife.

4. Sprinkle over the glitter.

5. Set aside until the icing hardens.

6. Enjoy!

How to make a footprint ghost!

Have fun making a ghost picture with your feet! This can get messy, so remember to put down a protective sheet, or create your picture outside.

What you will need:

- ★ Large sheet of black or coloured paper
- ★ Washable white paint
- ★ Sponge or paintbrush
- ★ Felt-tip pens
- ★ Water and kitchen roll/ a towel to clean your feet afterwards
- ★ A grown-up assistant to help

Method

1. Put your paper on the floor—make sure it can't blow away!

2. Paint the bottom of one foot using the sponge or paintbrush.

3. Step down on the paper, then carefully lift your foot away, trying not to smudge. Use a grown-up to help you balance.

4. Clean your foot!

5. Wait for your footprint to dry.

6. Once it is dry, get creative
    with your felt-tip pens!
    Draw on a face, maybe
    a bow like Luna's, and
    anything else you think a
    ghost needs.

How to make your own binoculars

Mirabelle takes her binoculars to hunt for the dragongrass flower. Here's how to make a pair for your own flower hunt!

What you will need:

★ 2 empty toilet roll tubes

★ PVA glue

★ Sellotape

★ Paper

★ Hole punch

★ String or ribbon

★ Decorating tools of your choice—pens, crayons, stickers, wrapping paper, or more

★ Scissors

★ A grown-up assistant to help

Method:

1. Lay the toilet roll tubes side by side and use glue to stick them together. Allow the glue to dry. (Alternatively, stick them together with sellotape.)

2. Take your paper and wrap it around the tubes, securing the end with glue.

3. Get decorating! You could use paint, stickers, wrapping paper, whatever you choose! Why not try drawing stars in purple or black to match Mirabelle?

4. Now to add a strap so you can wear them around your neck! Get a grown-up to help you punch a hole on the outside edge of each tube, just below the top.

5. Measure the string or ribbon so the binoculars will sit where you want them to.

6. Thread the string through the hole, and tie a knot in the end to secure.

7. Repeat with the other end of the string.

8. Time to explore! What flowers will you spot on your own hunt?

Spot these on a flower walk

Now you've got some binoculars ready for your flower hunt, why not see what else you can spot?

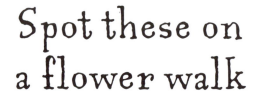

spiders

leaves

mushrooms

butterflies

bees

trees

dragonflies

flowers

Quiz

Which character from the story
should you dress up as for Halloween?
Take the quiz to find out.

1. Which Halloween activity do you like best?

A. Trick-or-treating with friends.

B. Carving pumpkins.

C. Watching spooky movies and telling ghost stories.

2. What's your favourite Halloween treat?

A. Jelly sweets.

B. Bonfire toffee.

C. Chocolate bars.

3. Which Halloween costume would you choose?

A. Witch or wizard.

B. Dragon.

C. Ghost.

Results

Mostly As
You should dress up as Mirabelle! You love to have fun with your friends and are always up for an adventure.

Mostly Bs
You should dress up as Violet the dragon! You're creative and full of energy.

Mostly Cs
You should dress up like Luna the ghost! You enjoy a good scare and have a mischievous side.

Harriet Muncaster

Harriet Muncaster, that's me! I'm the
author and illustrator of the Isadora Moon,
Mirabelle, and Emerald series.
I love anything teeny tiny, anything starry,
and everything glittery.

To visit Harriet Muncaster's
website, visit
harrietmuncaster.co.uk

From the world of ISADORA MOON

MIRABELLE

Gets up to Mischief

Half witch, half fairy, totally naughty!

Harriet Muncaster

From the world of ISADORA MOON

MIRABELLE

Has a Bad Day

Half witch, half fairy, totally naughty!

Harriet Muncaster

From the world of ISADORA MOON

MIRABELLE

Breaks the Rules

Half witch, half fairy, totally naughty!

Harriet Muncaster

From the world of ISADORA MOON

MIRABELLE

in Double Trouble

Half witch, half fairy, totally naughty!

Harriet Muncaster

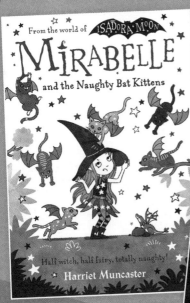

From the world of ISADORA MOON
Mirabelle
and the Naughty Bat Kittens
Half witch, half fairy, totally naughty!
Harriet Muncaster

From the world of ISADORA MOON
Mirabelle
and the Magical Mayhem
Half witch, half fairy, totally naughty!
Harriet Muncaster

From the world of ISADORA MOON
Mirabelle
Takes Charge
Half witch, half fairy, totally naughty!
Harriet Muncaster

From the world of ISADORA MOON
Mirabelle
Wants to Win
Half witch, half fairy, totally naughty!
Harriet Muncaster

ISADORA MOON

ISADORA MOON
Goes to School
Half vampire, half fairy, totally unique!
Harriet Muncaster

ISADORA MOON
Goes Camping
Half vampire, half fairy, totally unique!
Harriet Muncaster

ISADORA MOON
Has a Birthday
Half vampire, half fairy, totally unique!
Harriet Muncaster

ISADORA MOON
Goes to the Ballet
Half vampire, half fairy, totally unique!
Harriet Muncaster

ISADORA MOON

Gets in Trouble

Half vampire, half fairy, totally unique!

Harriet Muncaster

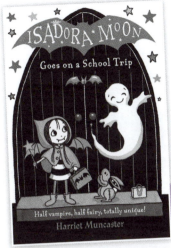

ISADORA MOON

Goes on a School Trip

Half vampire, half fairy, totally unique!

Harriet Muncaster

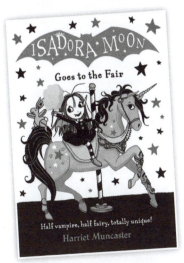

ISADORA MOON

Goes to the Fair

Half vampire, half fairy, totally unique!

Harriet Muncaster

ISADORA MOON

Makes Winter Magic

Half vampire, half fairy, totally unique!

Harriet Muncaster

ISADORA MOON
Has a Sleepover

Half vampire, half fairy, totally unique!
Harriet Muncaster

ISADORA MOON
Puts on a Show

Half vampire, half fairy, totally unique!
Harriet Muncaster

ISADORA MOON
Goes on Holiday

Half vampire, half fairy, totally unique!
Harriet Muncaster

ISADORA MOON
Goes to a Wedding

Half vampire, half fairy, totally unique!
Harriet Muncaster

ISADORA MOON
Meets the Tooth Fairy

Half vampire, half fairy, totally unique!
Harriet Muncaster

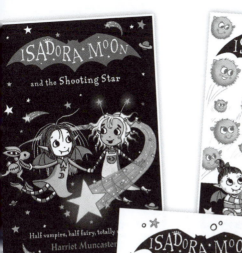

ISADORA MOON

and the Shooting Star

Half vampire, half fairy, totally unique!
Harriet Muncaster

ISADORA MOON

Gets the Magic Pox

totally unique!
Muncaster

ISADORA MOON

Under the Sea

Plus Isadorable activities

ISADORA MOON

and the New Girl

Half vampire, half fairy, totally unique!
Harriet Muncaster

ISADORA MOON

and the Frost Festival

Half vampire, half fairy, totally unique!
Harriet Muncaster

mpire, half fairy, to
Harriet Munca

Get ready to meet
Isadora's mermaid
friend, Emerald!

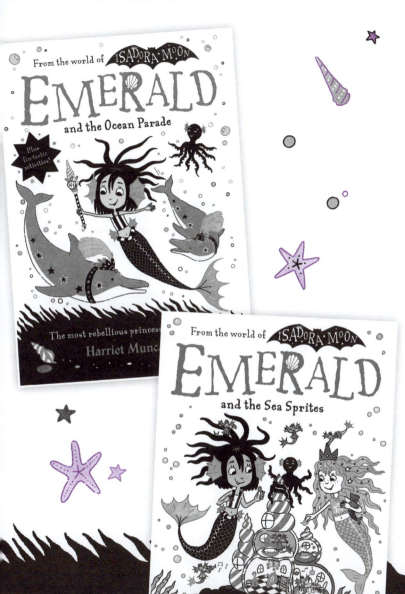

Like Mirabelle?
Why not try . . .

'sublime'
The Times

PiPPi
Longstocking

Astrid Lindgren   *Illustrated by Lauren Child*

SUIT UP. STEP UP.
IT'S TIME TO BECOME A HERO!

MARV
AND THE
**KILLER
PLANTS**

WRITTEN BY
ALEX FALASE-KOYA

PICTURES BY
PAULA BOWLES

Kitty
and the
Snowball Bandit

Plus
Superhero
activities!

Girl by day. Cat by night. Ready for adventure.

Written by **Paula Harrison** • *Illustrated by* **Jenny Løvlie**

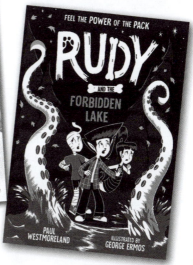

FEEL THE POWER OF THE PACK

RUDY
AND THE
**FORBIDDEN
LAKE**

**PAUL
WESTMORELAND**

ILLUSTRATED BY
GEORGE ERMOS